GET INFORMED—STAY INFORMED

Nationalism

Natalie Hyde

A Crabtree Forest Book

Crabtree Publishing

crabtreebooks.com

Crabtree Publishing

crabtreebooks.com 800-387-7650

 In Canada: We acknowledge the financial support of the Government of Canada through the Canada Book Fund for our publishing activities.

Author: Natalie Hyde
Series research and development: Reagan Miller
Editor-in-chief: Kathy Middleton
Editor: Ellen Rodger
Proofreader: Wendy Scavuzzo
Project coordinator: Melissa Boyce
Graphic design: Katherine Berti
Photo research: Natalie Hyde, Katherine Berti

Hardcover	978-1-0398-1519-3
Paperback	978-1-0398-1545-2
Ebook (pdf)	978-1-0398-1597-1
Epub	978-1-0398-1571-1

Printed in the U.S.A./072023/CG20230214

Library and Archives Canada Cataloguing in Publication

Available at Library and Archives Canada

Library of Congress Cataloging-in-Publication Data

Available at the Library of Congress

Published in Canada
Crabtree Publishing
616 Welland Avenue
St. Catharines, Ontario
L2M 5V6

Published in the United States
Crabtree Publishing
347 Fifth Avenue
Suite 1402-145
New York, NY 10016

Cover images:
Top: Flemish nationalists light flares in Brussels, Belgium, in December 2018 during a violent protest against a UN agreement on migration.
Bottom left: Banners in London, England, show support for Brexit, the United Kingdom's withdrawal from the European Union in January 2020.
Bottom right: Demonstrators in Toronto, Canada, carry pro-immigration signs to protest U.S. President Trump's immigration policies in January 2017.

Photographs and reproductions:
https://guides.lib.berkeley.edu/FreeResources/socialsciences—Screen Shot 2022-11-28 at 1.26.48 PM: p. 13 (inset bottom)
Shutterstock
360b: p. 35 (top)
a katz: p. 6
Alexandros Michailidis: p. 40–41, 43
Alexey Boldin: p. 15 (top)
Anjo Kan: p. 30–31 (bottom)
Antoni Mantorski: p. 8
Brian Minkoff: p. 38 (bottom)
Dizfoto: p. 27 (center)
Eric Crudup: p. 1
Everett Collection: p. 32 (both)
Hadrian: p. 16 (bottom)
Hang Dinh: p. 35 (bottom)
Ink Drop: p. 38–39 (top)
Jelani Photography: p. 14–15 (bottom)
johntallboy: p. 24
Luigi Morris: p. 31 (top)
meunierd: p. 5
Pradeep Gaurs: p. 27 (bottom)
Procyk Radek: p. 21
Rob Crandall: p. 17 (top)
Roshp: P. 37 (top)
Sergey Kamshylin: p. 13 (top)
VILTVART: p. 33
Wirestock Creations: p. 10 (bottom)
Yusron Motret: p. 23
Wikimedia Commons
Austrian National Library: p. 10 (top)
http://parismuseescollections.paris.fr:en:node:127343, Jean-Baptiste Lallemand: p. 7 (top)
Jinbo4514: p. 28 (bottom)
JLogan: p. 37 (bottom)
National Palace Museum: p. 28 (top)
Theuergarten Ewald: p. 34
Uwe Brodrecht: p. 25
Yahoo: p. 36 (top)
All other images by Shutterstock

Diagrams: Katherine Berti

CONTENTS

1 NEED TO KNOW

Nationalism is often viewed as the natural love for one's homeland. But it has come to mean many more things than that. Nationalism is a system of idea that is strongly influenced by history and culture. Sometimes it contributes to positive feelings of identity for a group of people who share a country or an ethnic background. At other times, it can influence people into thinking their race, **ethnicity**, or country is better than others. Taken further, it can result in hate and violence.

FORMS AND EXPRESSIONS

Walking down a street in Houston, Texas, visitors to the city may see hats and T-shirts with the slogan "American First." Bumper stickers, mugs, and stickers declare America should be made "Great Again." In the province of Quebec, Canada, the blue-and-white provincial flag is much more widely flown than the red-and-white Canadian flag. The provincial flag, the Fleurdelisé, represents Quebec's distinct French history, language, and culture. It dates back centuries. Beginning in the 1960s, it also became a symbol of Quebec nationalism or **cultural belonging** at a time of great change. A nationalist political movement which began at the time, called the "**sovereignty** movement," sought to separate the province from Canada and create an **independent** country. While the movement was at its peak in 1995, "Quebec first, Canada second," is still strong today. Nationalism and how it is expressed, or demonstrated, often changes over time.

QUESTIONS TO ASK

Within this book are three types of boxes with questions to help your critical thinking about nationalism. The icons will help you identify them.

THE CENTRAL ISSUES

Learning about the main points of information.

WHAT'S AT STAKE

Helping you determine how the issue will affect you.

ASK YOUR OWN QUESTIONS

Prompts to address gaps in your understanding.

▼ Quebecers celebrate Fête nationale du Québec on June 24. Fête nationale means "national festival." Quebec was recognized as a nation within a united Canada in 2006 by the House of Commons.

Symbols such as flags and emblems, and slogans such as "Make America Great Again," or "Le Québec aux Québécois" (Quebec for Quebecers), are examples of nationalism. Often nationalism is misnamed as patriotism. Although there are some similarities, there are distinct differences as well. Nationalism is a support for a nation, region, or group. Sometimes this means to the **exclusion** of the interests of others. It often stresses the importance of being "first" or "best." This is different from patriotism. Patriotism is the positive feeling about, and loyalty to, one's country or region. Patriotism can be as simple as standing for a national anthem, or learning about your country's core values.

▲ Nationalism is about belonging. Some forms of nationalism emphasize ethnic belonging. Others focus on political belonging. Some combine the two.

▲ The French Revolution (1789–1799) was a period of radical struggle and change. Revolutionaries fought for freedom from the absolute rule of a king.

> *It is not easy to see how the more extreme forms of nationalism can long survive when men have seen the Earth in its true perspective as a single small globe against the stars.*
>
> Arthur C. Clarke, science fiction writer

MODERN NATIONALISM

Many historians believe modern nationalism began in France, during the French Revolution. France's ruler after the revolution, Napoleon Bonaparte, spread the idea that France's culture and ideals were better than those of other countries. He claimed that France had the right to invade other countries to spread their superior ideals.

◄ Nationalist symbols are important for a feeling of unity. During the French Revolution, many people could not read or write. Wearing the tri-color cockade on their hats or coats identified them to others and made them feel united.

So, why should we care about nationalism? Some people argue that strong nationalism has been the spark that created movements for freedom and justice. They point to the American and French Revolutions. These conflicts were formed by groups of people who believed that their nation could be stronger, fairer, and more unified.

THE DARK SIDE?

Others believe nationalism has a darker side. They say it contributes to racism and divides society. People worry that it promotes conflict and is used by certain politicians to gain and maintain power. It promotes the idea that the nation has different responsibilities to its citizens than to its non-citizens. Critics point to violence around an "us versus them" attitude. This is especially true regarding immigrants. Even among citizens, it ranks them in importance based on race, religion, language, and wealth.

Knowing that nationalism can create harsh and unfriendly conditions between groups of people or between nations, it is important that we are aware of it and understand it. Nationalism is changing our world—in trade, **economics**, communities, and society. In our daily lives, we can see the effects on laws, travel restrictions, and **discrimination**.

▶ In October 2019, protestors demonstrated in front of the Turkish Embassy in London, England, over the Turkish violence toward Kurds. Kurdish language, clothing, and even names were banned by the majority Turkish people in areas where Kurdish people lived.

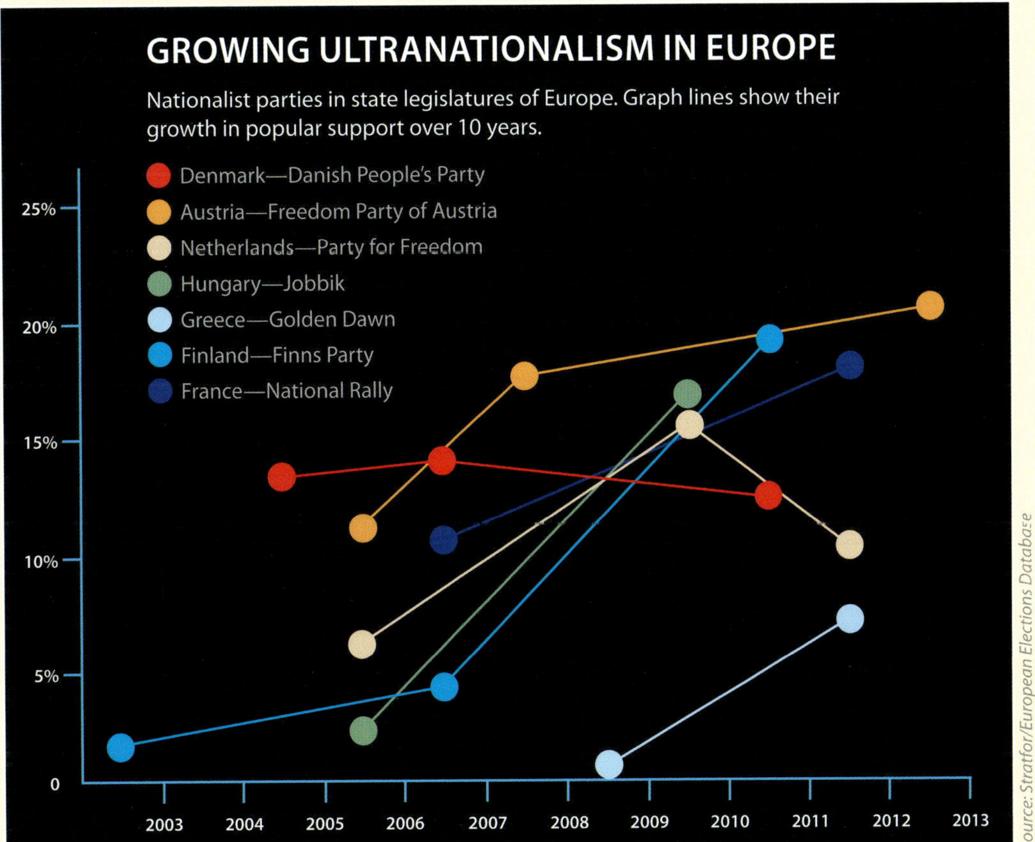

UNDERSTANDING INFORMATION

Accurate and up-to-date information can help us make good decisions. These decisions help us avoid the trap of seeing other groups of people as enemies. It can alert us to areas of the world where nationalism may erupt into violence or conflict. It can inform us when we are able to vote for representatives in our schools, clubs, sports, or society. In this book, we will learn how to get informed about nationalism. Examining how nationalism has grown and changed will help with understanding the good and bad sides of nationalism. This includes analyzing how symbols and slogans are used to spread ideas and beliefs. This will also allow us to find ways to stay informed and keep up with changes and risks.

2 HOW TO GET INFORMED

Exclusionary forms of nationalism are on the rise around the world. As more nations declare their goals to focus solely on their needs, wealth, trade, and borders, other nations begin to respond similarly. People and governments are then less willing to help other nations if it might affect their own aims.

> *Nationalism, in my opinion, is nothing more than an idealistic rationalization for militarism and **aggression**.*
>
> Albert Einstein, physicist

All issues have different sides. Nationalism is no different. One side includes those who believe nationalism will keep their country safer and more secure, and its citizens healthier and wealthier. The other side sees nationalism as a threat to world peace and the ability to work on global problems such as pollution, terrorism, and climate change. Understanding the key players, background information, and the vocabulary that you will come across is **vital**. Key players in the issue of nationalism are world leaders, activists, and politicians.

BACKGROUND INFORMATION

Background information on how nationalism has helped or harmed other countries through history will allow us to understand what results may come from modern nationalism. Knowing the vocabulary found in articles or news programs that relate to nationalism is important. Some words such as **isolationist** or **chauvinism** may be unfamiliar to you. Understanding what you are hearing or reading will help you get informed on the topic.

Reading current news reports and articles is a good way to figure out who the key players are on the world stage. History websites or books on revolutions and conflicts are one way of understanding how and when nationalism played a part in conflicts, peace, or changing borders. Online searches of dictionaries and vocabulary lists are good places to start to get familiar with new words.

THE CENTRAL ISSUES

Does an increase in nationalism around the world mean a high risk of conflict between nations?

▼ While much of today's learning is done online, not all books have digital copies. Libraries are still an excellent way of finding background information.

◀ Librarians can direct you to many different sources for research.

Getting informed on a new topic means finding information in source material. Source material can be things that are written, visual, auditory, or as artifacts. Written source material is the most common and includes books, documents, reports, articles, journals, and even pamphlets. Visual sources can be paintings, photos, or posters. Audio sources can be recorded interviews or music. Artifacts are human-made things that give information such as sculptures, **architecture**, ceramic bowls, or wooden carvings.

Different types of sources are found in different places. Libraries, **archives**, government offices, or the Internet have lots of written sources. Art galleries, exhibits, or even personal photo albums can store visual information. Many recordings and music are available digitally. Artifacts can be kept formally in a museum or informally in someone's home. Source material is all around us.

KEY INFORMATION

Primary sources are the original creators or owners of information, for example, a journal kept by a soldier fighting in WWI.

Secondary sources are reports, analyses, and interpretations of the primary sources, for example, a magazine article about the effect immigrants have on the job market.

Tertiary sources are summaries or databases of primary and secondary information. They include Wikipedia articles or entries in encyclopedias.

Everyone has their own way of looking at and making sense of the world. Opinions and beliefs also play a part in how we might record or create source material. This slant or focus in source material is called "bias." Bias can be obvious, such as a rant against a certain country's customs. It can also be subtle, such as a hint or slight mention of the limitations of a certain culture. But all forms of bias can color what information is created and how it is presented. Bias is not necessarily bad, but it is important that we recognize it so we can factor that into conclusions we draw from it.

▶ Job records created during World War II in **Nazi Germany** can give insight into things such as the background of workers, their names, working conditions, and travel restrictions.

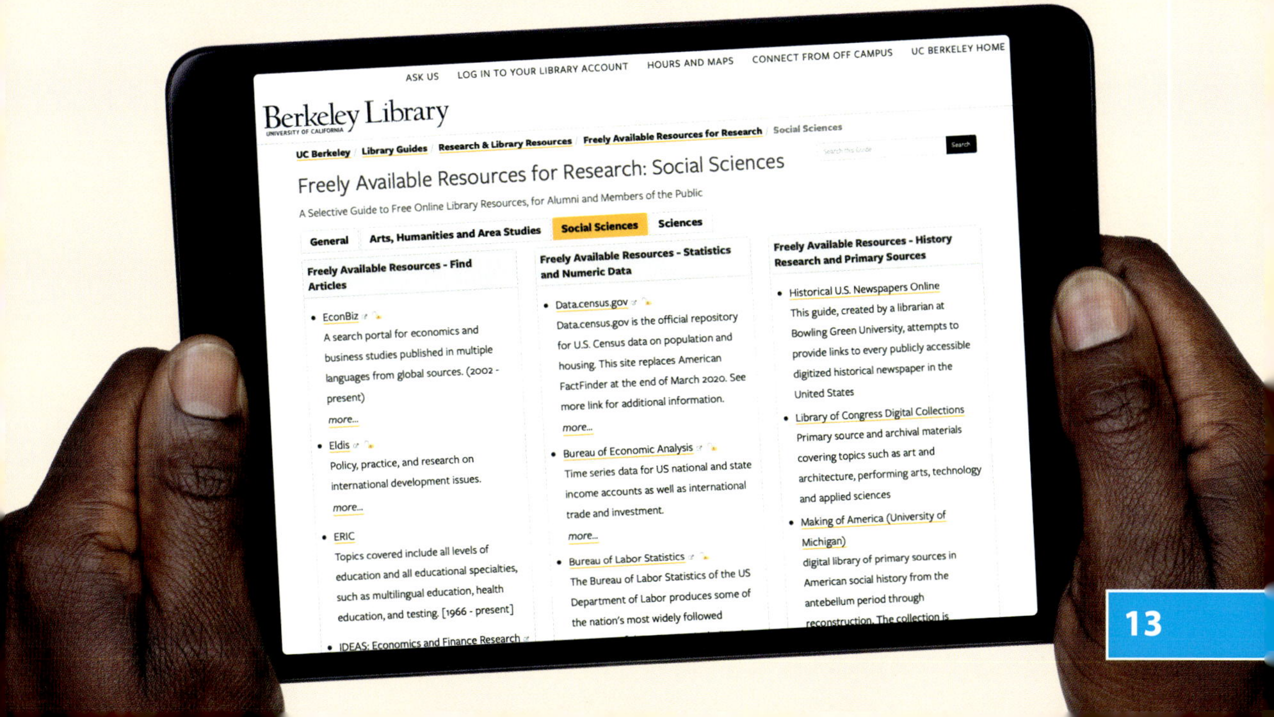

With so much data to discover, it is important to learn how to find and judge reliable information. Fake news, **conspiracy theories**, and exaggerated facts are risks when researching any topic. This is especially true when using the Internet where anyone can make a professional-looking website and post content that supports their views.

TIME AND PLACE RULE

Many historians use the Time and Place Rule. This rule states that the closer to the original event the source material is created, the more likely it is to be accurate and reliable. An interview with a war survivor just after a conflict will be more accurate than a feature article on an anniversary of the war. This sometimes means finding source material near the location of an event is necessary. Searching for historical sites, government offices, or local libraries may lead to valuable source material.

Beyond the Time and Place Rule, it is also important to look at the **credentials** and background of the authors or creators of source material. Some people call themselves experts when they don't have the education or background to support that claim. Google searches of the creator can give surprising results. For experts, find out what papers they have published and what universities they may have studied at or worked for.

ASK YOUR OWN QUESTIONS

To determine if a source is credible, consider:

- Does the creator have solid credentials and expertise in the topic?
- Does the headline match the story?
- Is the publisher known to be reliable?
- What sources did the creator use?
- Is the source relevant and up to date?
- Is the source meant to be a joke or clickbait?

▶ Interviews done while an event is happening, such as this protestor at the "Stop the Steal" event in 2020, are a good example of the Time and Place Rule for information.

▶ Wikipedia is a source of general information. But because anyone can edit information on any of the pages, it should be used with caution.

3 NATIONALISM

Nationalism and patriotism are not the same thing. The term "patriotism" was first used in the 1600s to refer to a patriot who was devoted to and loved his country. Patriotism is seeing your own country in a positive way. The word "nationalism" was first used in the 1900s and originally meant roughly the same thing.

It was after World War II (WWII) that the word "nationalism" started to have a negative meaning. In Nazi Germany, people were encouraged to believe that Germany was unique and the German people were special. The idea was that their culture, language, and race were superior to others. This belief allowed the Nazi **regime** to justify any behavior, as long as it supported these ideas.

This is the danger of today's extreme or ultra nationalism. People are united based on their shared background. Nationalism can be based on language, ethnicity, or religion. Nationalists do not like any sort of **criticism** about their country, even if it is true. People who do not fit into their definition of national identity are excluded. This leads to groups pushing for laws and policies that favor their country in trade, immigration, and **tariffs**.

▼ The "**America First**" policies caused the US to end trade agreements that had been in place for years and try to **renegotiate** them to better benefit the US.

▲ Voting in elections, flying a flag on a home or business, serving in the military or honoring soldiers, and working to improve your neighborhood or country are concrete examples of actions motivated by patriotism.

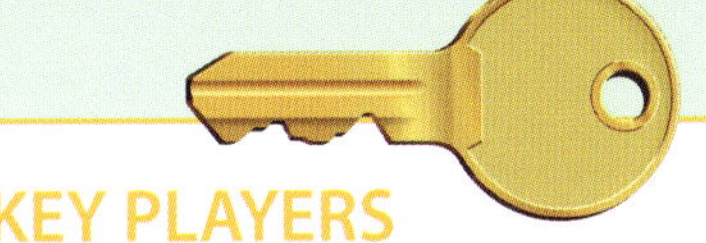

KEY PLAYERS

The Parti Québécois is the political party in Quebec, Canada. It's primary goal is to get independence for the province of Quebec and make it a sovereign state. It considers its French-Quebec identity, including language and culture, as special and unique. It put its nationalism to a vote in 1994, but was narrowly defeated.

> "*The difference between patriotism and nationalism is that the patriot is proud of his country what it does, and the nationalist is proud of his country no matter what it does.*"
>
> Sydney J. Harris, American Journalist

Almost every issue has both positive and negative sides. Nationalism is no different. It can have some **beneficial** effects on a nation's identity. When citizens feel a common bond, it can affect how they behave toward each other and toward other countries.

Almost all nations are made up of groups with different backgrounds, languages, and religions. When there is a national identity, these different groups can feel united. This is true in the Philippines. The Philippines is a group of islands in Southeast Asia. There are more than 130 different ethnic groups living there. According to the public opinion company YouGov, the Philippines is ranked as the seventh most nationalistic country in the world.

Nationalism can also help people work for a shared common good. Finland is ranked the 13th most nationalist country in the world. In Finland, there is a common goal to rid the country of homelessness. Housing is being provided to all residents who need support in a program called "Housing First."

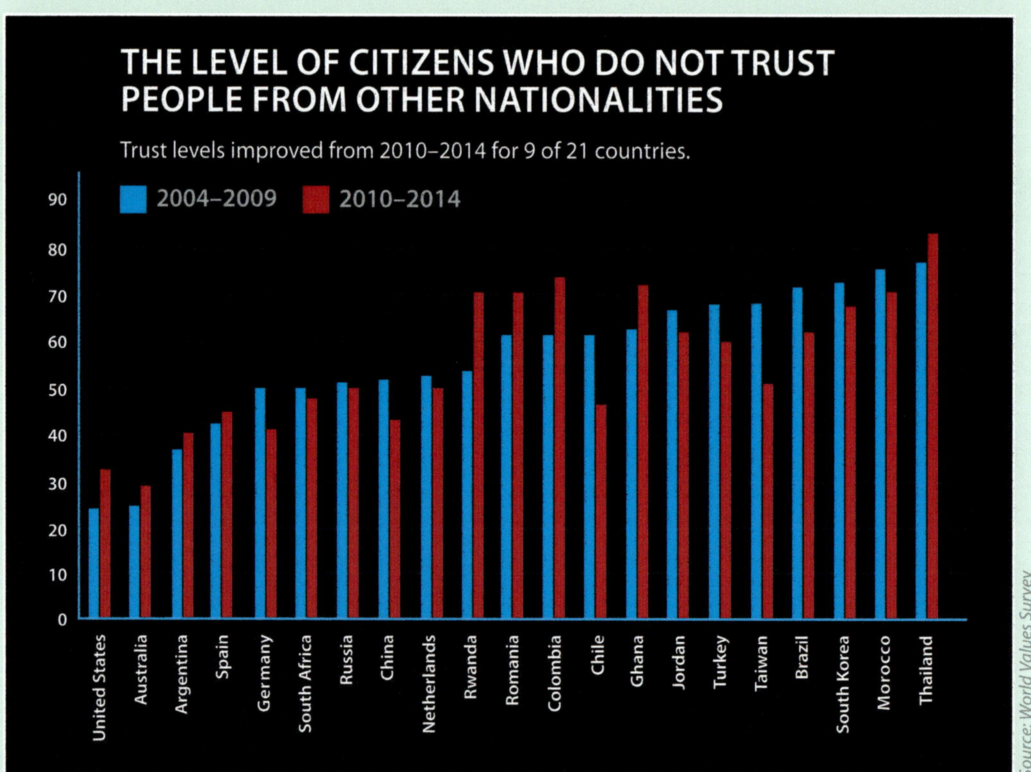

Source: World Values Survey

▲ Ukrainian troops wear blue and gold identifying flags on their uniforms. The country was invaded by Russia in 2014 and again in 2022.

In countries that are more nationalistic, citizens tend to be less concerned about paying taxes. This is because they see their taxes as working to improve the lives of all citizens. Norway is one of the highest-taxed countries in the world. Its citizens are also ranked the happiest in the world. People there are mostly content to pay higher taxes because they feel they are getting a better lifestyle for it. They have **universal health care**, low-cost education, and good working conditions. Fifty-nine percent of Norwegians believe that their country is "better than most."

Nationalism is also a driving force during war and conflicts. Citizens band together to fight a common enemy. This can be seen in the invasion of Ukraine by Russian forces in 2022. Ukraine is a country of many different ethnic groups. At a time of conflict, the Ukrainian flag and colors were symbols of a united people fighting a common enemy.

NEGATIVE NATIONALISM

The strong feelings citizens might have for their nation can have a negative side. While nationalism can create a sense of unity within a nation, it can create a separation from the rest of the world. Focusing on only promoting one nation's health, wealth, and advantages has a ripple effect around the world.

Nationalism leads to people believing that only one nation's needs are important. This results in short-sighted agreements and **alliances**. Trade with other countries is vital to ensure the spread of goods and services. Fuel and power are good examples of this. When Russia invaded Ukraine, it also cut oil and gas supplies to Europe. This was intended as punishment for European countries helping Ukraine. Without oil and gas, Europeans struggled to heat their homes, have power, or use their vehicles. Nationalism in Russia led the government to base its decisions solely on what would benefit Russia.

PROTECTING INTERESTS

Some nationalists feel justified in doing whatever it takes to support or protect the interests of their country. This can include hurting people of other countries through conflict, unfavorable trade agreements, and limiting immigration. In 2011, when civil war broke out in Syria, in the Middle East, millions of Syrians fled the country. Hungary was one of the countries that closed its borders to refugees. Hungary has strong nationalistic feelings with its leader as a member of the Our Homeland Movement. This movement supports among other things, separating Hungarian and **Roma** children in schools.

▼ During the Russia-Ukraine conflict, Russia shut off the main gas pipeline to Germany. It claimed a leak caused the closure, but Germany accused Russia of using energy as a weapon.

WHAT'S AT STAKE?

What types of world events might make you feel more nationalistic toward your country? What types would lessen your feelings of nationalism?

HUNGARY'S NATIONALISM

During the height of the Syrian war in 2015, **asylum** seekers fled to Europe to escape violence. Most European countries gave them refuge. About 390,000 crossed into Hungary. Most were Muslim. The nationalist government of Hungary set up high fences and closed the border. Hungary then passed a series of anti-immigration laws. As a member of the **European Union** (EU), Hungary was asked to find homes for 1,294 refugees. It refused. Hungary's leader, Viktor Orbán asked voters to "defend Christian values and Hungarian national identity" because his government feared Hungary would become "a breeding ground for terrorism." Many Syrian refugees were charged with illegal border crossing and held in jail. In 2022, at the beginning of Russia's invasion of Ukraine, refugees from Ukraine were welcomed into Hungary. Ukrainian refugees are European. Most have a Christian background.

Globalism is the idea that we are all connected in ways that disregard borders. Nations should work together toward common goals and common good. This includes trade agreements, and fighting global problems such as pollution and climate change.

Nationalism's "us versus them" ideas lead to separating people into groups such as "naturals vs foreigners," "fit from unfit," and "internal safety vs threats from other nations." It tends to see other countries as competitors instead of **allies**. Globalism is the idea that nations depending on each other and working together improves the economy of all of them. Countries in the European Union, such as Germany, France, and Spain, have agreements that allow citizens to work in the other countries. This means all countries benefit from having the best workers.

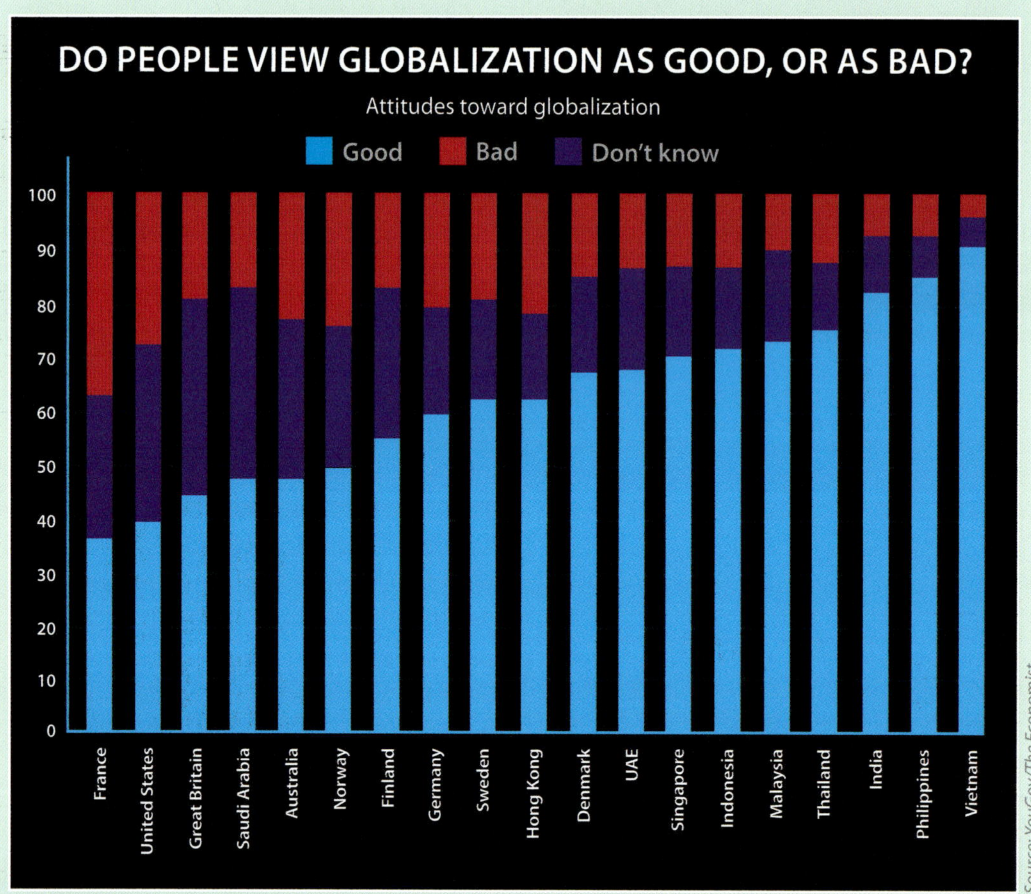

▲ Dr. Tedros Adhanom Ghebreyesus, director general of the World Health Organization, speaks to the World Democracy Forum in 2020. COVID-19 presented a challenge to all countries to work together.

The **COVID-19 pandemic** showed examples of both nationalism and globalism. At the beginning of the pandemic, supplies of personal protective equipment (PPE) such as masks, gowns, and gloves around the world quickly ran out. Some countries began **hoarding** PPE so their medical workers were protected. Health care workers in less-developed countries struggled to safely treat the virus.

On the other hand, at the same time, scientists around the world worked together to develop a vaccine as quickly as possible. They shared data and procedures and it was the fastest a vaccine has ever been developed, tested, and offered to the public. It has changed how vaccines will be developed in the future. Unfortunately, nationalism took over after the vaccine was developed. Countries tried to secure doses for their own citizens first, leaving some nations without. It was a short-sighted reaction because with a virus that traveled the world, immunity in all countries is necessary to control its spread.

There are different factors that can lead to a country's citizens developing a feeling of nationalism. Governments often encourage nationalism because it can maintain support for its actions, policies, and laws. Countries that are eager to control and restrict their population use nationalism to instill fear of outsiders in its citizens. In North Korea, the government makes a point of describing other countries as enemies to fear. It controls all educational material as well as the media, including the Internet. This allows the North Korean government to constantly feed its citizens a news diet of misinformation.

SOCIAL MEDIA'S ROLE

Social media is another factor in growing nationalism. People share their opinions and beliefs, even if they are not founded in facts. This allows half-truths and **distorted** data to **circulate**. People who do not carefully research what they read can be misled. Some online posts are deliberately created to sow the seeds of mistrust in other groups. This can unite people against what they see as a threat to their lifestyle.

Often a nation's own history comes into play. Countries such as India have been invaded, conquered, and **inhabited** more than 200 times in history. The idea that the nation has to band together to fight off other cultures wanting to take over can unite people behind nationalism. But India's nationalism is also rooted in religion. In 1947, India was split into two countries: India and Pakistan. Pakistan became a homeland for Muslims and India became a Hindu-majority state. Each country's identity is very closely tied to the main religion of the nation.

THE CENTRAL ISSUES

Would an increase in the number of global trade agreements around the world reduce growing nationalism? How?

▶ This open-air TV screen in North Korea, like all TVs in the country, can only broadcast television stations run by the state. This means the government can control all information reaching the people. North Korea is a country governed by a dictatorship. The government promotes a type of nationalism in which the state and the North Korean people are the same. This is reinforced by government **propaganda**. Disagreeing with the state would mean betraying the people.

People and governments often use symbols to express their nationalism. Colors, flags, clothing, and slogans are powerful ways to send a message. This helps the message spread, even to people who don't speak the same language or can't read.

A powerful nationalist symbol is a wall. It **conveys** the idea that anything outside a country's borders is a threat. The Berlin Wall was built in 1961. It separated East Berlin, which was in the control of the **Soviet Union**, from West Berlin, which was part of West Germany. It was made of concrete and almost 14 feet (4.2 m) high. It was a visual reminder of the separation between the two halves of the city and how citizens were not free to travel back and forth. Walls have been used in other areas to restrict immigrants and refugees. But walls are more symbolic than practical. Most illegal immigrants and drug smugglers do not rely on trying to sneak over a wall to cross a border.

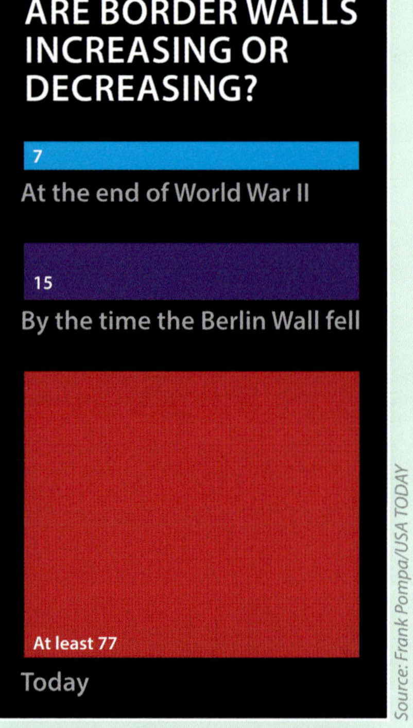

Source: Frank Pompa/USA TODAY

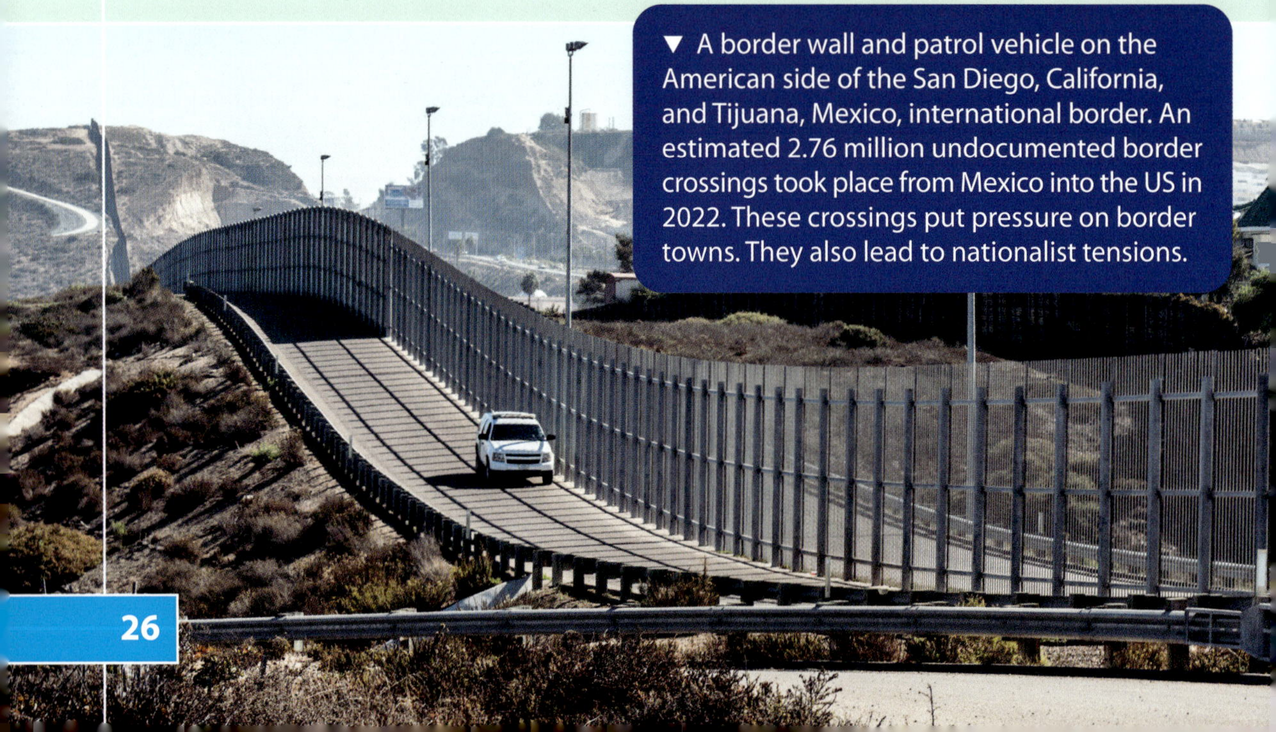

▼ A border wall and patrol vehicle on the American side of the San Diego, California, and Tijuana, Mexico, international border. An estimated 2.76 million undocumented border crossings took place from Mexico into the US in 2022. These crossings put pressure on border towns. They also lead to nationalist tensions.

ASK YOUR OWN QUESTIONS

Do statistics show that border walls work to keep illegal immigrants or smugglers out of a country? Where can you find out?

▲ Swastikas are ancient symbols still used by South Asian cultures to represent good luck. Nazi Germany adopted the swastika as a symbol of the "master race."

EXTREME NATIONALISM

Extreme or ultra nationalist groups often turn to symbols so they can recognize each other and state their beliefs in a non-verbal way. Sometimes symbols are taken from foreign or ancient cultures, then their meanings are changed. The swastika that came to represent Nazi Germany was first used as a sacred religious symbol more than 7,000 years ago. It was only when the Nazis began using it that it came to represent a perceived superior race of white Europeans.

Hats, T-shirts, and pins with certain colors and slogans can be used to **intimidate** others or bring other people over to their cause. Uniforms are another powerful symbol of a country and its strength. The military of a nationalistic government often has a distinctive uniform meant to intimidate and control the public.

▼ The Rashtriya Swayamseva Sangh (RSS) is an Indian Hindu nationalist **paramilitary** group. One of its members assassinated **Mahatma Gandhi** in 1948, partly because Gandhi talked of religious tolerance.

4 NATIONALISM AND HISTORY

An identity that fuels nationalism is often rooted in history. Stories about a glorious past with successes and victories promote pride in a nation. But these feelings move from patriotism to nationalism when people begin to think that these successes are due to a superior culture, race, language, or religion.

Nationalism sometimes begins with the idea that all the people in a country descend from one common ancestor. In Mongolia, a large number of men can trace their lineage back to the great warrior, Genghis Khan. Mongolian nationalism is infused with the idea that the country should include land that was part of Khan's Mongol Empire. It has helped unite people toward that goal.

England has its own national myth in King Arthur. This legendary figure was a great leader and warrior. More importantly, he had a code of morals and values that included honor, **chivalry**, and justice. The legend of King Arthur has become such a symbol of Great Britain that it has inspired researchers and **archaeologists** to research sites to investigate the roots of the myth and determine whether there are any facts to back it up.

Fictional legends and myths are often used by nationalist leaders and groups to inspire followers. And archaeological research has been used in propaganda. Findings are sometimes distorted to support the story people want to be true. Artifacts are sometimes used to link a modern group of people with impressive historical deeds or events. Iraqi nationalists, for example, claim archaeological links with the ancient civilizations of Sumer and Babylon.

Genghis Khan

King Arthur

▶ Iraq's former dictator Saddam Hussein saw himself as a modern Nebuchadnezzar the Great. Nebuchadnezzar was an ancient king of Babylon whose territory included what is now modern Iraq. He was the most powerful ruler in the world. Hussein tried to used archaeology to promote his nationalist views. He spent millions building a reconstructed Babylon in the 1980s—on top of the ancient city's ruins. His aim was to illustrate how powerful he, and modern Iraq, were.

▼ Hussein tried to make his modern Babylon in the model of the ancient one. He even had his name pressed into building bricks.

> *Nationalism makes us weak because its eternal seeking of enemies...makes cooperation with other nations...much more difficult.*
>
> Frans Timmermans, Vice-President of the European Commission

The feeling that a nation and its history and culture belong to a certain group a people is a core belief of nationalism. That means other people wanting to move into the country are seen as foreigners and not "true citizens." Not welcoming immigrants and refugees is one of the problems of strong nationalism.

Nationalistic countries tend to have stricter limits on immigration. Immigrants are feared to be a burden on the country's economy and budget. Another belief is that these newcomers will take jobs away from citizens. These citizens are often angry at their government for using public money to care for immigrants and refugees.

NATIONALISM AND BELONGING

During the Syrian civil war, a flood of refugees made its way into many European countries. More than 1.25 million people wanted to claim asylum in 2015. The large number of people put these countries into financial crisis in order to care for them. Nationalism in European countries rose as more and more refugees arrived. Some Syrian refugees claim the Greek coast guard forced their boats back into open water so they could not land. Greek officials dismiss the claims, saying the coast guard was working at their top ability to try to keep up.

Other countries welcome immigrants and refugees. Chile is a country in South America. It has taken in hundreds of thousands of refugees from the South American country of Venezuela. Venezuela is in the middle of political and economic crisis. As the number of migrants increased, opposition from anti-migrant groups increased as well. Some Chileans believe the migrants are more likely to be criminals. But most migrants just want to work and build a future in a more stable country.

KEY PLAYERS

Nigel Farage was the leader of the Brexit Party (United Kingdom Independence Party) in the UK. His party used slogans such as "Go it alone" and "Break Free" to convince the British to leave the European Union. His party encouraged nationalism with images of lines of immigrants, and data to create fear and mistrust. After the successful vote to leave the EU, Farage resigned.

▶ Millions of Syrian refugees live in Turkey. Many took dinghy boats from there to Greece. The pressures of admitting and caring for large numbers of refugees can inflame nationalist tensions in refugee-receiving countries.

▶ Protestors gather in New York City in August 2021 to demand the US accept all Afghan people seeking asylum. As of January 2022, more than 68,000 Afghans have relocated to the US.

Nationalism can lead to cruelty and neglect of certain groups who don't fit in with the national identity. Sometimes this is a targeted program to rid the country of ethnic or religious groups. This often includes threats, violence, and even mass murder, called "genocide."

An extreme form of nationalism developed in Nazi Germany (1933–1945). Nazis defined white, "Nordic", or ethnically German Christians as part of a "master race." All others were inferior races. The Nazis used death camps to murder Jews, Roma, and Slavic peoples, as well as others deemed "undesirable." Nazi nationalist ideology was used to convince Germans that these people were responsible for many problems facing the country. This belief meant ordinary people turned a blind eye to what was happening. It also meant officers felt justified in carrying out orders for mass killings.

ASK YOUR OWN QUESTIONS

What is the difference between ethnic cleansing and normal warfare? What is the end goal of ethnic cleansing?

◀ Extreme forms of nationalism can be used to convince populations that they are "superior" to others. Six million Jews were murdered by the Nazi regime during the Holocaust.

▼ Ukrainians stand with images of the 1932–1933 Holodomor, to call attention to the dangers of ethnic nationalism and ideologies that can result in mass killings. They fear Russia is promoting similar forms of nationalism in its war on Ukraine today, including denying that Ukrainians are a distinct people.

TERROR AND NATIONALISM

It is a terrible reality that the Nazis were not the only government to commit such crimes. There were several genocides before the Holocaust. Today, many countries, including the US and Canada, recognize the Ukrainian Holodomor of 1932–1933 as a genocide, or deliberate mass murder of Ukrainians. The Holodomor is also known as the Terror Famine. Ukraine's land had been collectivized, or made into communal, or group farms by the Soviet Union beginning in the late 1920s. In 1932 and 1933, Soviet leader Josef Stalin sought to control Ukrainians by increasing farm quotas on grain and cutting back on food allotted to farm workers. The quotas were followed by other measures intended to wipe out Ukrainians and Ukrainian resistance to Soviet rule. The resulting genocide cost an estimated 3.9 million Ukrainians their lives. More died of disease, or when they were deported, or forced from their homes into other areas of the Soviet Union.

The belief that a nation is superior to others can lead to an **erosion** of justice. When laws are not applied to all groups equally, those who are labeled as "others" can fall victim to more roadblocks for opportunities. They might also be targeted for arrests and harsher punishments.

Leaders who stress hard-line forms of nationalism will often lie and distort the truth. Their exaggerations are a way to sway public opinion. With the public on their side, they can do whatever they want. This includes ethnic cleansing to make the nation "pure," and promoting the interests of people considered true nationals. Nationalistic leaders will also use fear and threats to keep people from coming forward with facts or complaints.

Nazi Germany's leader, Adolf Hitler, used this approach during WWII. He lied about the violence and aggression against the Jewish people. The Nazis created a fake attack on a German radio station to justify their invasion of Poland. If anyone dared to speak the truth about what was going on, Hitler accused them of spreading lies. This confusion about what was true and what were lies allowed the Nazis to go ahead with their plans. They lied about the genocide of Jews by saying they were being resettled in new areas.

▶ A Nazi propaganda poster promotes the Volksempfänger, a radio developed in 1933 at the request of Nazi Minister of Propaganda, Joseph Goebbels. The radio was tool Goebbels used to spread Nazi nationalism and to incite listeners to follow their will.

▲ A sign on a tram says "Only for German Passengers." These were used on the entrances to public transit, parks, and buildings. It was just one example of the extreme nationalism of the Nazi regime.

Nationalistic leaders often break the law if it gets in the way of their ambitions. They will justify their actions by saying it was for the good of the nation. They will also claim that the laws themselves are unfair and they deserve special treatment. They will try to control the media, including television, radio, and social media. If they can control the message, they can bend the rules in their favor. In North Korea, only government-controlled stations are broadcast. This allows the government to hide its real agenda and convince the public that they are better off than other nations.

▼ Sometimes leaders try to downplay dissent by appealing to nationalism. When thousands of Egyptians gathered in Tahrir Square in 2011 to protest then president Hosni Mubarak and his policies, Mubarak tried to hold onto power by insisting the protestors were foreign agents and not Egyptian citizens at all.

5 WHERE THINGS STAND

In recent years, countries were focused on globalism. The idea was to build a connected world for trade, travel, jobs, and justice. The belief was that this would bring development and growth all around the world. But nationalism is now on the rise.

There are many reasons why nationalism is growing and crises help it along. One more recent crisis is the COVID-19 pandemic. Border closures and travel restrictions kept citizens at home during the pandemic. Governments needed help to control the spread of the virus and asked people to act for "the public good." This strengthened the feeling of belonging to a united group. Companies also urged citizens to support local jobs by buying goods produced in their own country.

But during this world crisis, some countries also increased "me first" thinking. Many scrambled to get medical supplies, vaccines, and equipment. The pandemic highlighted weaknesses in international organizations and agreements. The COVID-19 Vaccine Global Access (COVAX) program was created to distribute vaccines equally around the world. However, it was often short of supplies. Countries capable of creating vaccines kept more for their own citizens than they sent to the program, leaving developing countries with **shortfalls**. This was called "vaccine nationalism."

The pandemic has also resulted in many countries focusing on the idea of self-sufficiency. Self-sufficiency means a country produces the goods and services it needs within its borders. There is less need to rely on trade with other countries. But there will always be the need to work with other countries.

"*Nationalism is a tool increasingly used by leaders to bolster their authority, especially amid difficult economic and political conditions.*"

Richard N. Haass, American diplomat

ASK YOUR OWN QUESTIONS

What are the policies and factors that show a government is encouraging globalization over nationalism?

◀ People in India wait for limited supplies of the COVID-19 vaccine. Even though India had production plants for two different vaccines, most of the supply was exported to other countries.

Nationalism turns the focus of a country inward. It can be used for good, or for evil—especially if fear and suspicion about other countries and their motives grows. It is not surprising, then, that its increase might result in the breakup of international alliances.

After WWII, countries in Europe began making economic and customs agreements with each other. Seeing the benefits of working together, more countries wanted to make stronger connections. The European Union was created in 1993 with 12 founding member states. They included the United Kingdom, Belgium, Denmark, Germany, Ireland, Greece, Spain, France, Italy, Luxembourg, the Netherlands, and Portugal. The agreement created a central European bank, a common **currency** known as the euro, and security policies.

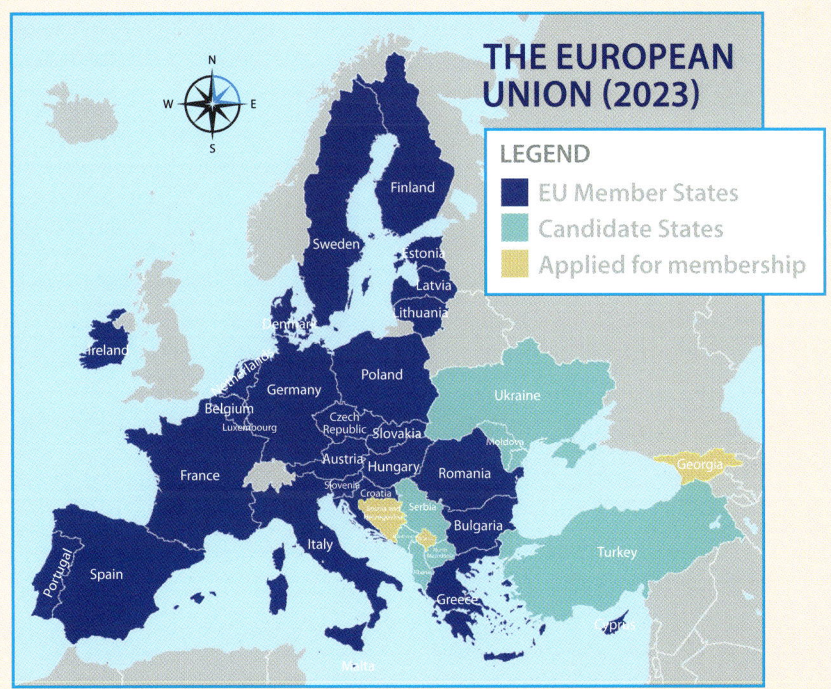

The United Kingdom was an original EU member nation. However, rising nationalism combined with discontent over poor economic performance led people there to question whether being a member of the EU was the best route for the country. A movement to leave the EU, called "Brexit," was formed. One key player in encouraging anti-EU feelings was Nigel Farage. As head of the United Kingdom Independence Party (UKIP), he encouraged British nationalism with descriptions of immigration problems, trade restrictions, and terrorist threats. In a vote in 2016, more than half the population agreed to leave the EU.

WHOSE INTERESTS?

While two-thirds of Europeans have positive feelings toward the EU, some nationalist political parties are gaining support. The Rassemblement National (RN) in Belgium and the AfD (Alternative fur Deutschland) in Germany are two of these parties. Even though statistics show that the EU has benefited all members, many people think the EU might be gone in 20 years. Many Europeans fear the result of the EU collapsing would be mostly negative. They think it would hamper their ability to trade, travel, and work in other EU countries.

▶ In 2019, supporters in London, England, hold signs supporting Brexit. Brexit is the name given to Great Britain's nationalistic decision to leave the European Union.

▲ Nigel Farage left UKIP in 2018. He then formed the Reform UK party.

LEAVE
MEANS
LEAVE
NO DEAL?
NO PROBLEM!
LEAVEMEANSLEAVE.EU
PERCENTAGE OF PEOPLE IN EUROPEAN COUNTRIES WHO THINK THE EU WILL BE GONE IN THE NEXT 10–20 YEARS
70%
60%
50%
40%
30%
20%
10%
0%
Slovakia
France
Romania
Poland
Italy
Greece
Czech Rep.
Hungary
Netherlands
Germany
Austria
Sweden
Denmark
Spain
Source: ECFR-YouGov survey

6 KEEPING UP TO DATE

Getting informed about a topic means building a knowledge base. Staying informed requires continually researching, reading, and reviewing old and new ideas about the topic. Libraries are perfect places to find information in books, magazines, journals, and on the Internet.

Sometimes it is hard to distinguish facts, or even to find information that explains a situation clearly. When you do find information, it is important to examine the subject from different angles. Be open to questioning your own biases.

Because nationalism is often viewed as negative, sometimes its presence is hidden. Nationalist governments who want to control what information reaches the public will not make facts and figures easily available. Many carefully control or edit what the public sees, reads, and hears. Other times, nationalism is given another, less negative name, such as "patriotism." This is why understanding key vocabulary is so important.

> "*We are all living together on a single planet, which is threatened by our own actions. And if you don't have some kind of global cooperation, nationalism is just not on the right level to tackle the problems, whether it's climate change or whether it's technological disruption.*"
>
> Yuval Noah Harari, Professor, Hebrew University of Jerusalem

SEARCH TIPS

When looking at websites, address extensions can help pinpoint what sort of information you may be getting.

.gov (government)—restricted to use by government entities.
.org (organization)—anyone can register for this, although it is often used for nonprofit organizations and charities.
.com (commercial)—originally for businesses, it is the most widely used extension.
Country extensions:
.ca Canada
.au Australia
.uk United Kingdom
.ru Russia
.de Germany

In search windows on the Internet:

- Use quotation marks around a phrase to search for that exact combination of words (for example, "Syrian refugees").
- Use the word Define and a colon to search for word definitions (for example, Define: discrimination).
- Use a colon and an extension to search a specific site (for example, European Union:.gov for all government websites that mention the European Union).

▼ Golden Dawn is an extreme nationalist group in Greece. Here, supporters celebrate getting members elected to government in Greece. Golden Dawn became a political party in the country in 1993. Members hold racist views, support fascism, oppose immigration, and are anti-globalization.

◀ More than 8 in 10 Americans get their news from digital devices. Almost half of Americans admit they often get news from social media.

WHOSE INTERESTS?

When researching nationalist groups, be aware that some are open about their goals. They will be proud of their efforts to change laws or protest government action. Their aims will be found with a quick Internet search. You will have to dig a little deeper when information is missing. Asking questions is a good way to learn what you need to know. Checking with a librarian can help. They can guide you in how to search for information.

Not all source material is created equal. It is important to check where you are getting your information. Look at the dates on statistics. Search for the backgrounds of organizations or groups to figure out their aims and goals.

Remember, all source material will have some bias. By recognizing that bias, you can determine how the data might be slanted to prove one viewpoint or another. Try to find a balanced view. Read and watch reports by both sides. On the topic of nationalism, this might be information put forward by think tanks, protest groups, and also government offices. In social media, you might read blogs both for and against new laws or policies that might be influenced by nationalism.

Check the facts given in articles, blogs, reports, and videos. Even reliable sources sometimes give false data accidentally. Try to find two or more sources that give the same percentages, or the same facts. Look to institutions that are not tied to one side or the other for balanced data.

Make it easy for yourself to keep up to date. These days, there are lots of ways to do this online. You can use search engine alerts, such as Google alerts, to inform you of when a new article on a topic is posted. News **aggregator sites** use programs to search the Internet for news items on a single topic. They gather all types of news events and happenings on one page, making it easier for you to stay informed and save time.

▲ Nationalism affects lives around the world and can lead to war, internal conflict, trade disputes, and travel restrictions. Flemish nationalists in Belgium protest a United Nations pact for safe, orderly, and regular migration of people in 2018. Extreme or ultra nationalists often oppose or want to put strict limits on immigration.

GLOSSARY

aggregator sites Sites that collect data from other sources across the Internet

aggression Hostile or violent behavior toward another

alliances Agreements made between countries or organizations

allies Other countries that help and cooperate with a nation

America First US government policy that promoted nationalist ideas during the 1920s, and again during the presidency of Donald Trump (2017–2021)

archaeologists Scientists who study human history through artifacts

architecture Designing and constructing buildings

archives A place where documents and records are stored

asylum Protection, shelter, and support for those who have left their country

beneficial Favorable or good

chauvinism Extra support for your own gender, country, or group

chivalry The religious, moral, and social rule for medieval knights

circulate Move through a loop

conspiracy theories Beliefs that an event is a secret plot by powerful people

conveys Makes known

COVID-19 A contagious disease caused by a virus that caused a pandemic (2020–) and led to more than 6.7 million deaths worldwide

credentials Qualifications and achievements

criticism Analyzing and judging something negatively

cultural belonging The part of a person's identity that is related to their nationality, where they live, and their culture

currency The system of money used by a country

discrimination Unjust treatment of certain people or groups

distorted Twisted out of shape

economics The production and movement of wealth

erosion Wearing away

ethnicity The common culture, language, or traditions of a certain group of people

European Union A political association of 27 countries in Europe

exclusion Being left out

exclusionary Tending to exclude

hoarding Collecting and keeping more than you need

independent Not being ruled or controlled by others

inhabited Lived in or occupied by someone or a group of people

intimidate Frighten

isolationist A person who believes in a national policy of not getting involved in political or economic relationships with other countries

Mahatma Gandhi An Indian lawyer and political and human rights activist who was dedicated to non-violent action. He is considered a Father of the Nation in India.

Nazi Germany The German state controlled by the fascist Nazi party from 1933–1945

pandemic An outbreak of a disease that affects the whole world

paramilitary Unofficial forces organized like a military force

propaganda Misleading information used to support a certain political view

regime A government in power, especially an authoritarian one

renegotiate To discuss the terms of an agreement again to make improvements

Roma An ethnic group throughout Europe who have often been persecuted

shortfalls Amounts that are less than expected

sovereignty A country's power to govern itself

tariffs Taxes on imported or exported goods

universal health care State- or government-supplied health care that everyone in a country has access to, paid through their tax dollars

vital Absolutely necessary

SOURCE NOTES

QUOTATIONS

Page 7: Clarke, Arthur C. *The Exploration of Space. Pocket Books Inc, 1951*, p. 187.
Page 10: Einstein, Albert: https://bit.ly/3XD0LQQ
Page 17: Harris, Sydney J. *Strictly Personal*. H. Regnery Company, 1953.
Page 29: Timmermans, Frans: https://bit.ly/3QQ2MH3
Page 36: Haass, Richard: https://bit.ly/3HgdyTM
Page 40: Harari, Yuval Noah: https://bit.ly/3wy6ZWR

REFERENCES USED FOR THIS BOOK

Chapter 1: Need to Know, pp. 4–9
https://bit.ly/3ku4BNV
https://wapo.st/3XD8dMp
https://bit.ly/3CZ5fte

Chapter 2: How to Get Informed, pp. 10–15
https://bit.ly/3iNsqQb
https://bit.ly/3wcD4De
https://bit.ly/3wfpAH2
https://bit.ly/3XDWVqA

Chapter 3: Nationalism, pp. 16–27
https://bit.ly/3ZL1Fwv
https://www.ukip.org
https://brook.gs/2ONBt2N
https://bit.ly/3ZEOOvl
https://econ.st/3WsgwJb
https://bit.ly/2K7QJFm

Chapter 4: Nationalism and History, pp. 28–35
https://bit.ly/3koyVJM
https://bit.ly/2PZ4eWJ
https://www.pbs.org/tpt/dictators-playbook/episodes/saddam-hussein
https://www.wmf.org/project/future-babylon
https://bit.ly/3ZVnfOZ
https://bit.ly/3ZX0MRx
https://www.jstor.org/stable/1404182

Chapter 5: Where Things Stand, pp. 36–39
https://cpj.org/2015/04/10-most-censored-countries
https://econ.st/3HiHWNG
https://bit.ly/3HdvC11

Chapter 6: Keeping Up to Date, pp. 42–43
http://factcheck.org
https://bit.ly/2LgzeQa
https://guides.lib.uw.edu/research/faq/reliable

FIND OUT MORE

Finding good source material on the Internet can sometimes be a challenge. When analyzing how reliable the information is, consider these points:

- Who is the author of the page? Is it an expert in the field, or a person who experienced the event?

- Is the site well known and up to date? A page that has not been updated for several years probably has out-of-date information.

- Can you verify the facts with another site? Always double-check information.

- Have you checked all possible sites? Don't just look on the first page a search engine provides.

- Remember to try government sites and research papers.

- Have you recorded website addresses and names? Keep this data so you can backtrack later and verify the information you want to use.

WEBSITES

Look into the rise of nationalism with Academic Kids: **https://academickids.com/encyclopedia/index.php/Nationalism**

Find out with DK how Hitler convinced a nation to follow him: **www.dkfindout.com/us/history/world-war-ii/adolf-hitler**

Meet young immigrants and learn their stories with Scholastic: **https://bit.ly/3XF9x1n**

BOOKS

Baby Professor. *What Are the Countries in the European Union?* Baby Professor, 2017.

Mooney, Carla. *The Holocaust: Racism and Genocide in World War II*. Nomad Press, 2017.

Portus, Sam. *Fascism: Radical Nationalism*. Mason Crest, 2018.

ABOUT THE AUTHOR

Natalie Hyde has written more than 100 fiction and non-fiction books for young readers. She lives in a rural area with her husband and children.

INDEX

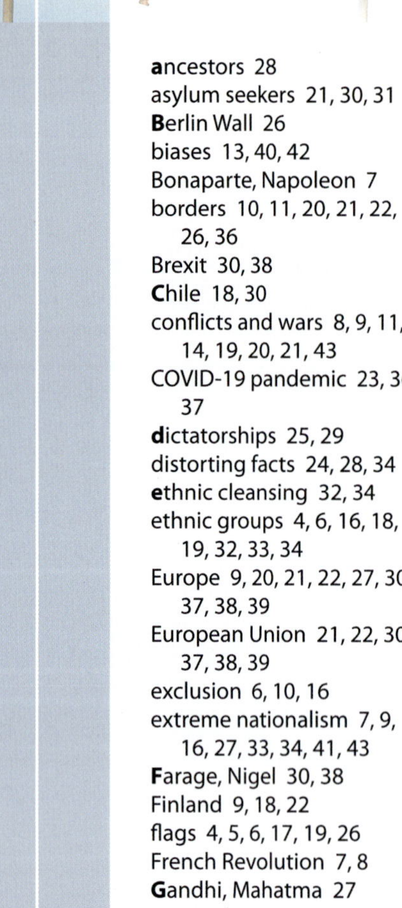